I Watched my Brother Being Born!

Including Children at Birth

Written by Anne Vondruska and daughter Katarina Vondruska
Pictures by Christy Scherrer and Patricia Williams
Artwork by Katarina Vondruska

Order this book online at www.trafford.com
or email orders@trafford.com

Most Trafford titles are also available at major online book retailers.

Printed in the United States of America.

ISBN: 978-1-4120-7277-9 (sc)

Trafford rev. 01/05/2015

www.trafford.com
North America & international
toll-free: 1 888 232 4444 (USA & Canada)
fax: 812 355 4082

For the Parents

My goal with this book is to teach our children that giving birth is a natural, safe and fulfilling process. Unless the birthing mother has an illness that needs special medical attention, it need not be treated as a disease.

By including our children at birth they can see that it is a normal and healthy physical event.

We should empower children with a healthy view on childbirth. If we instill in them at an early age that childbirth is as healthy as life gets, the new generation will make educated choices for themselves and their baby.

Medical advancements in the obstetrical field are great, but should be used only when needed. "Don't fix it if it's not broken." Most women are created in a perfect way to give birth, and we need to trust that.

My hope is that more people will talk to their children and educate them about natural, healthy childbirth. If your children's birth story is empowering, share it with them and they may one day share it with their own children. Better yet let them see their younger siblings being born. Letting them be part of such an important family event is something they will cherish and remember forever, and it may impact sibling bonding.

I do believe that a fair amount of preparation is needed. Reading books about birth, watching videos of real births as well as talking about the upcoming event is important. Also find out if there is any fear that you and your partner have, loss of intimacy, too loud, afraid to be naked in front of the children etc.

There is a lot to put into considerations such as who will be able to give full attention to the kids so it is not a distraction to the mother in labor. Other things to think of are the ages of the children, and have realistic goals that match their ages. There will also be different involvement if it is a day-time birth or night-time.

I have included suggested books and videos. My hope is that you also find this book and video helpful in educating your children about natural childbirth.

Good luck!

Many thanks!

Having my friend Patricia there for them, allowed Katarina and Magnus to be able to come and leave, as they wanted. I made it clear to them that if they did not want to watch the birth, they did not have to. I was also concerned that I would need some time where I could be with my husband without interruptions. I did not have to worry if they needed food, if they were bored, or just needed attention. My friend's job was to take care of the kids, but it was an extra bonus to have her as my massage-therapist. She even managed to take some pictures, and film. She is incredible.

I also had a doula at the birth named Andrea. Being a doula myself, I know the benefit of their support, and remembering how long and tiring my labor with my second child was I decided to at least be prepared for a long labor. Andrea is a wonderful doula with many years experience, and it shows. The energy and protection that I felt from all the women there was wonderful.

My husband, Tom was able to fully enjoy the birth of Christian. Having lots of experience with the two other births, he was now a veteran in catching babies. It was nice to feel his love and strong commitment to making us feel safe and protected. Having Katarina and Magnus there made our family-bond stronger and better than I ever thought possible. I am so blessed to have a husband that shares the same values and ideas about childbirth as I do.

Yelena Kolodji, CNM was our midwife for the previous two births, so it made a lot of sense to have her there for Christians birth too. Tom and I both have a lot of respect for her professionally and as a nice caring mother figure. Having the same midwife for all 3 children enhances the feeling of safety and familiarity. It is almost like having my mother there, who knows me so well. She knows my strengths and weaknesses better than anyone. Thanks to her and her birth team we had another peaceful and safe birth.

Without Christy Scherrer, my good friend and birth-photographer this book would never come to life. It would have been just another great memory, stored away in our brain. She has a great eye for capturing the right moments.

Last, but not least thank you to the many people that have taken the time to help me edit and suggest corrections to this book.

Anne Vondruska

It was December. I was so excited. It was more than Christmas this month. A baby was coming to our family. We were waiting for this big event to happen. Katarina is my name, and I am seven. My brother Magnus is five. I would like to tell you the story of how my brother was born.

My brother Magnus was extra excited because we had found out we were going to have a brother. My mommy had an ultrasound, and they had clearly seen a penis. He was jumping up and down, and finding toys he wanted to share with the new baby. He picked out many names. He was super happy. I was hoping we would have a sister, because then we could share a room. I was still very exited that we soon would have a little baby brother.

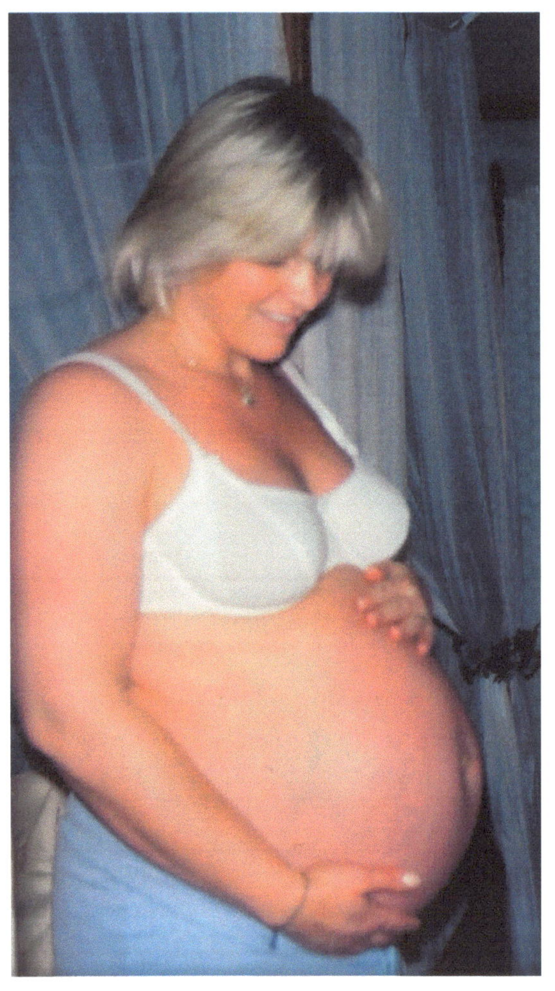

My Mommy's belly grew bigger and bigger. It looked a little funny, especially when she walked. It looked as if she had swallowed a whole watermelon and now it was stuck there.

Sometimes I went with my Mommy to visit the midwife. She lived in a forest, and her name was Yelena. The walls in her office were covered with pictures of babies she had helped deliver. There were pictures of both Magnus and me there. It was a lot of fun to look at those pictures. There were pictures of more than 300 babies hanging on the walls, and they were all so cute.

When Magnus and I went to Yelena's office, we would listen to the baby's heartbeat. We could also feel the baby move in Mommy's stomach. It was amazing to see the baby moving its feet. It was as if he were punching the inside of my Mommy's belly. Yelena helped me use a fetus scope to listen to the baby's heartbeat. Most of the time I was not able to hear anything, but with a doppler we could hear thump, thump, thump, thump... The midwife told me that the baby's heartbeat was faster than mine, and it was fun to check that out.

My Mommy watched movies with us about babies being born, and we also read lots of books. She told us that it was normal for the pregnant mother to use loud noises when she was in pain. She called it a birth song. I think it sounds a little like a hippopotamus crying for help. She said it was a sign that the baby would be born soon.

One day my Dad drove my brother and me to school. He told us that Mommy thought the baby would be born today, and that she needed quiet time before the baby would be born. It was very exciting when my Dad came to pick me up early from school. He said it was time to come home and be part of the big family event.

When I came home my Mommy was already in the Jacuzzi. She was having a doula keeping her company. My mom asked me if I wanted to join her, and I did not have to be asked twice. My brother did not want to come in. He seemed shy.

The night before there had been a rainstorm, but now at about one in the afternoon, there was not a trace of it left.

The sun was up and all the rain had dried. It was nice and warm. We spent over one hour outside in the warm Jacuzzi. My Mom liked being in water very much, and she was not screaming yet.

One of Mommy's friends was there to help take care of us! Her name is Patricia. She brought food from our favorite restaurant. I had chicken, mashed potatoes with gravy, and my favorite of all, green beans with garlic butter.

We made little figures out of play dough. I made a pink dog. Magnus made many different shapes, and even some snakes. I like making figures out of play dough.

We left Mommy and Daddy alone so they could take a shower. We walked to the park, and had a great time running and playing.

It must have been good for Mommy and Daddy to take a shower. When we came back they were dancing around, Mommy holding tight around Daddy's neck. My Mommy seemed to be working much harder now. She looked serious, and moved around faster.

She needed more help now, and I wanted to be helpful, so it was nice to give her some water to drink. I also put a cold washcloth on her forehead.

Magnus was also very helpful. He fed Mommy a banana, and also massaged her hands and arms.

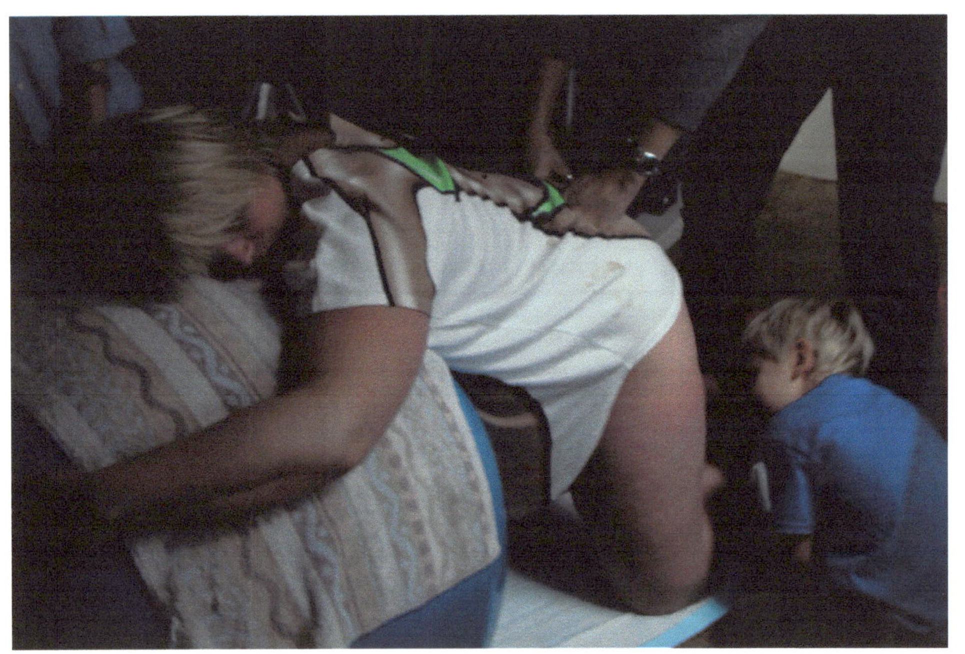

A few times Magnus would keep looking at my Mommy's bottom to see if the Baby would come soon.
He was a little impatient!

I was not afraid, because I knew my Mommy was very strong. She told us she was OK the whole time, so that way we didn't worry. Sometimes she would smile, but most of the time she had a serious face and looked like she was meditating.

Mommy really liked being in water, so she would spend a long time in the tub that was set up in the bedroom. She wanted to have the baby be born in water.

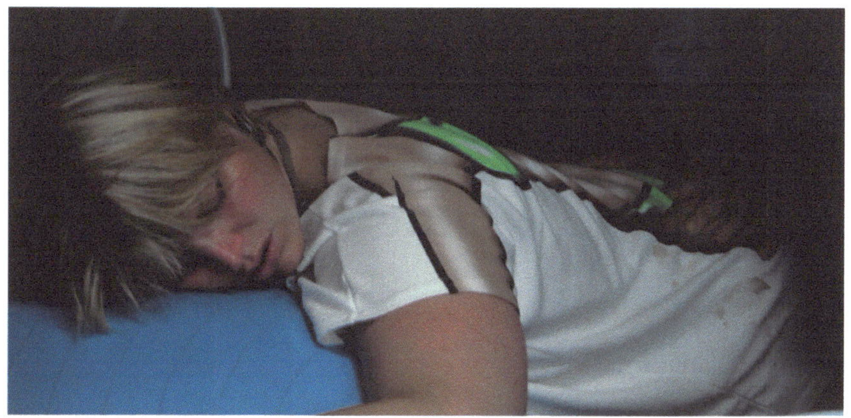

Mommy did not sit still or lay down for long. She said it hurt less when she was moving. She was leaning over a big, blue ball, rocking back and forth. Sometimes she would sit on the ball too.

Daddy was massaging her lower back. She said that felt nice and relaxing. Sometimes the midwife would give her a hug, or talk softly to her, "You are doing a great job!". My Mommy got a massage, but she had a hard time lying still, so soon she was up and working again.

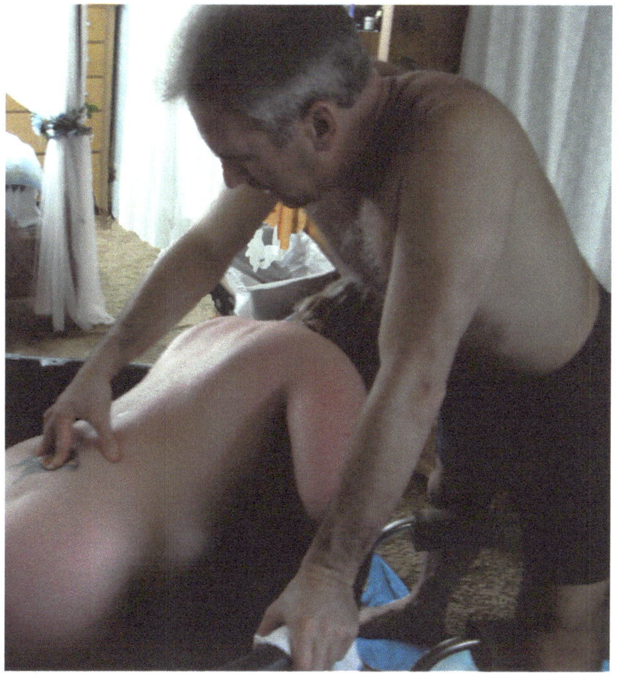

Yelena kept checking the baby's heartbeat many times during the labor just to reassure us that everything was normal and healthy. One time we had to leave the room. We got busy eating, and we squished play dough again. Sometimes I would listen through the closed door.

All of a sudden we heard Mommy getting louder. It sounded a little like the birth-song that we had waited for. We all rushed for the door not wanting to miss seeing our baby come. She squatted in the big tub of water, and we all watched as Mommy started to dance. At least that was what it looked like to me. It seemed like hard work. Suddenly we saw our baby's head pop through the water. Like a rocket the baby's whole body came out into the water. He was caught by my Daddy and handed over to my Mommy. He was a little purple, but mostly red. Mommy hardly used any loud noises at all. He was plump and little, and so cute.

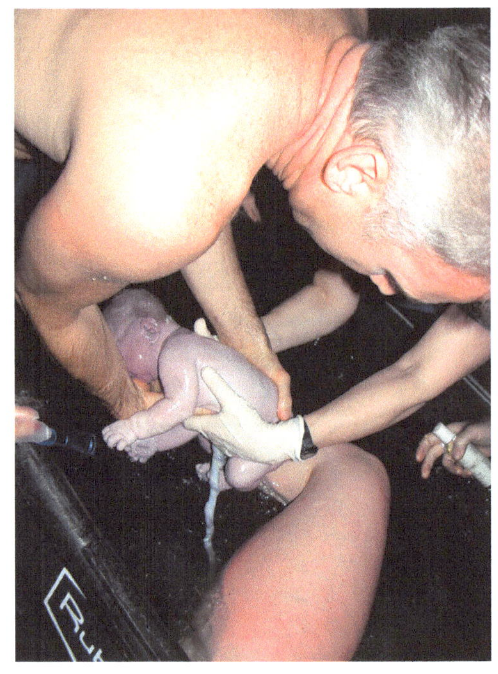

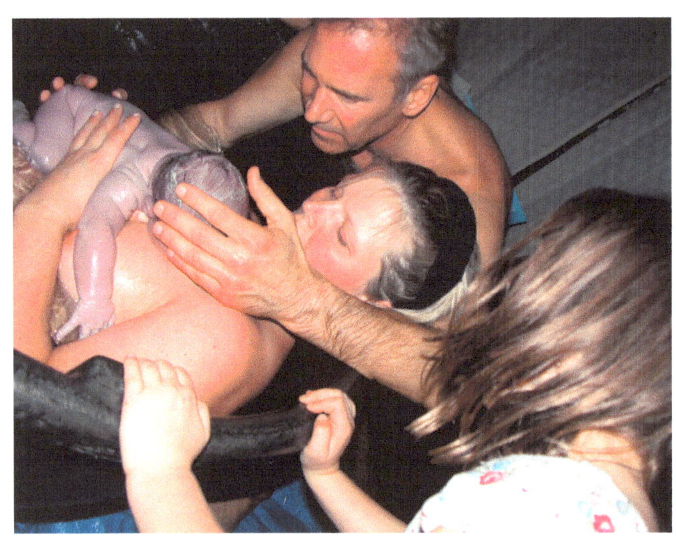

The baby was crying a lot. The midwife said that was a healthy sign. After 5-10 minutes Daddy helped Magnus cut the umbilicus-cord. I was busy watching, and amazed by what had just happened. I had a brand new baby brother.

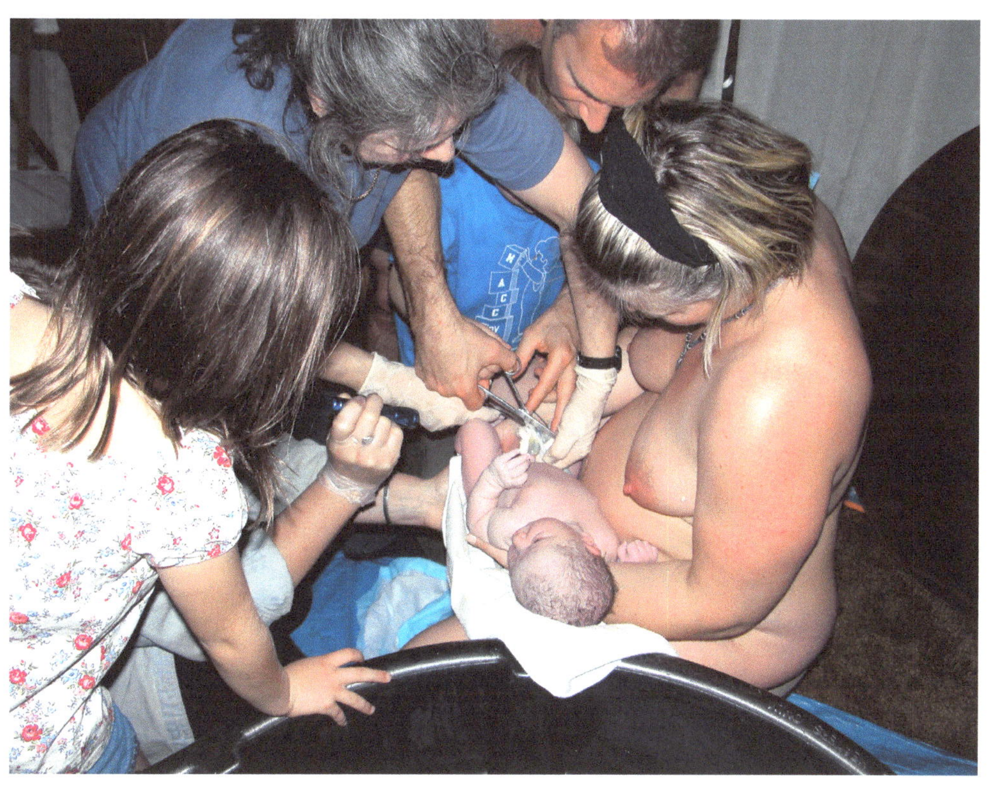

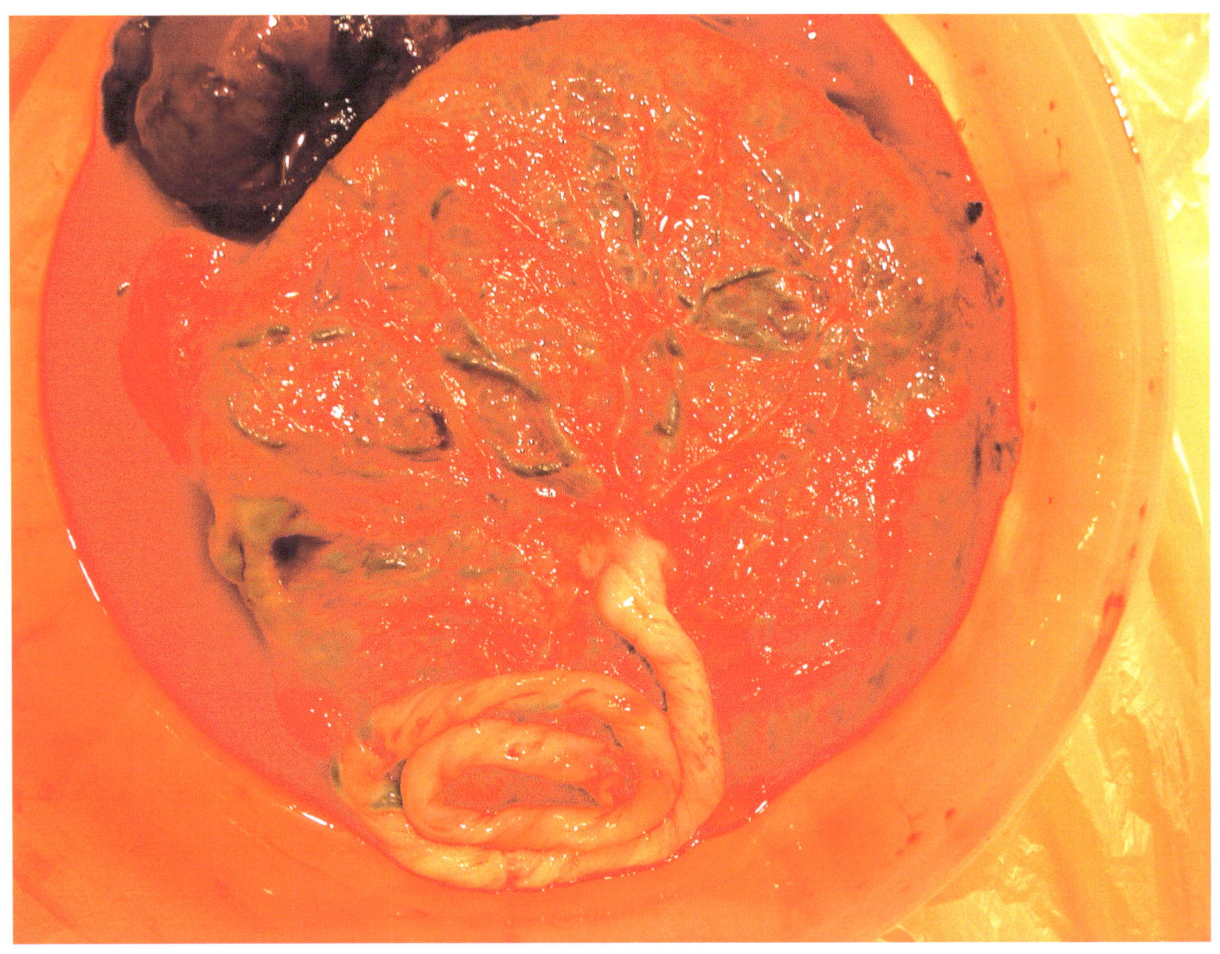

We looked at the placenta. It was smooth and shiny on one side, and rough and bumpy on the other side. It had a lot of lines going in all kinds of directions, and it looked like the roots on a tree. The midwife showed us this bag where the baby had been inside. It is amazing that our baby brother could fit into such a little space. The umbilicus-cord was longer than I thought it would be, and looked a little like a long telephone cord. Magnus said that the red color of the placenta was his favorite red color. Pink is still my favorite color.

I am so happy that I got to be there when my brother was born.

Now our brother is 20 months old and Magnus and I are also older. We both love our brother Christian so much, because he is funny, cute, and very lovable. He gives the greatest hugs.

Here are some books and videos that I found valuable to help prepare and educate my children for the birth. I specifically planned for a water-birth, but even if you are not planning to give birth in the water, these videos show real natural birth, and the noise, and intensity can help children become familiar with what it may look and sound like.

Book " From Conception to Birth" by Alexander Tsiaras
Book "Welcome with Love" by Jenni Overend
Video "Born in Water" 7 water births from the Andaluz Water Center
Video "Birth Day" with Naoli Vinaver Lopez and Family

You can get these videos and many more at www.BirthingTheFuture.com.

Welcome with love you can get at www.attachmentscatalog.com.

We also watched birth videos that I borrowed from my midwife's private library.

Dedicated to my Mother
who gave birth to me and
my three wonderful children.

A video with the same title is available at:
www.FamilyBirthing.net

Birthphotographer Christy Scherrer can be reached at:
www.bellymotherbaby.com

www.ingramcontent.com/pod-product-compliance
Ingram Content Group UK Ltd.
Pitfield, Milton Keynes, MK11 3LW, UK
UKHW060123300726
14090UKWH00002B/329
9781412072779